Sports Biographies

Wayne Gretzky
Hockey Star

Heather Feldman

Rigby®

Wayne Gretzky: Hockey Star
Copyright © 2001 by Rosen Book Works, Inc.

On Deck® Reading Libraries
Published by Rigby
1000 Hart Road
Barrington, IL 60010-2627
www.rigby.com

Book Design: Michael de Guzman
Text: Heather Feldman
Photo Credits: Cover © Rick Stewart/AllSport; p. 5 © Elsa Hasch/AllSport;
p. 7 © CP Picture Archive; pp. 9, 13, 17 © AllSport; p.11 © Todd
Warshaw/AllSport; p. 15 © Ian Tomlinson/AllSport; p. 19 ©
Corbis/Mitchell Gerber; p. 21 © Ezra Shaw/AllSport.

On Deck® is a trademark of Reed Elsevier Inc. registered
in the United States and/or other jurisdictions

06 05 04 03
10 9 8 7 6 5 4 3 2

Printed in China

ISBN 0-7635-7843-6

Contents

Meet Wayne Gretzky

Wayne Gretzky is
a hockey star.

Wayne started playing hockey when he was a young boy.

Number 99

When Wayne was 18 years old, he played for a team called the Edmonton Oilers. Wayne was number 99 for the Oilers.

Wayne played hockey for a lot of teams. He played for the Los Angeles Kings.

Wayne kept a hockey puck from a game. He played against the Oilers in the game and beat them!

Wayne also played for the New York Rangers. Wayne was number 99 for them, too.

The Stanley Cup

Wayne's teams won the Stanley Cup four times. The Stanley Cup is the most important prize in hockey.

Wayne loves to spend time with his family.

Wayne does not play hockey anymore. At his last game, he waved good-bye to his fans. Wayne will always be a hockey hero.

Glossary

puck (**puhk**) the hard, black rubber disk that players use in ice hockey

Stanley Cup (**stan**-lee **kuhp**) the prize given each year to the best hockey team

team (**teem**) people who play together on one of the sides in a game

Resources

Books

The Great Gretzky
by Ken Call
Grosset & Dunlap (2000)

Wayne Gretzky: Hockey Greats
by Thomas Raber
Lerner Publications (1999)

Web Site

The National Hockey League Web Site
http://www.nhl.com/kids

Index